D1613896

Voting: Rights and Suppression

Stuart A. Kallen

ReferencePoint Press®

San Diego, CA

For more information, contact:
ReferencePoint Press, Inc.
PO Box 27779
San Diego, CA 92198
www.ReferencePointPress.com

LIBRARY OF CONGRESS CATALOGING-IN-PUBLICATION DATA

Names: Kallen, Stuart A., 1955- author.
Title: Voting : rights and suppression / by Stuart A. Kallen.
Description: San Diego, CA : ReferencePoint Press, Inc., 2022. | Series:
  Challenges for democracy | Includes bibliographical references and
  index.
Identifiers: LCCN 2021055911 (print) | LCCN 2021055912 (ebook) | ISBN
  9781678203108 (library binding) | ISBN 9781678203115 (ebook)
Subjects: LCSH: Suffrage--United States--Juvenile literature. | Voter
  suppression--United States--Juvenile literature.
Classification: LCC JK1846 .K35 2022 (print) | LCC JK1846 (ebook) | DDC
  324.6/2--dc23/eng/20220325
LC record available at https://lccn.loc.gov/2021055911
LC ebook record available at https://lccn.loc.gov/2021055912

CONTENTS

Young Americans Have Low Opinion of US Democracy

American democracy has been experiencing many challenges. Foremost among those challenges is the widespread perception that US democracy is either "in trouble" or "failing." This is the view of a majority of young Americans, age eighteen to twenty-nine. A national poll conducted in Fall 2021 by the Harvard Kennedy School Institute of Politics finds that only 7 percent of young adults view the United States as a "healthy democracy."

Which of the following phrases best describes the United States today?

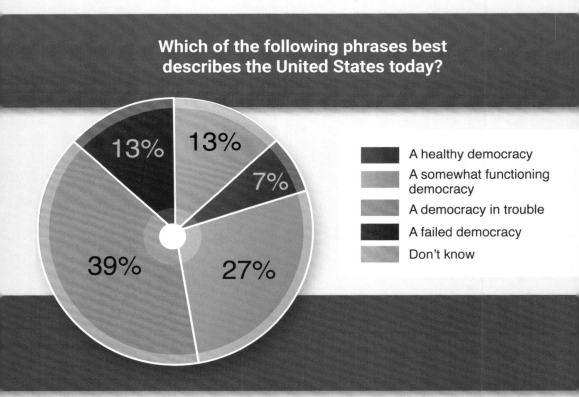

13%   13%

7%

39%   27%

- A healthy democracy
- A somewhat functioning democracy
- A democracy in trouble
- A failed democracy
- Don't know

Source: "Harvard Youth Poll," Harvard Kennedy School Institute of Politics, December 1, 2021. https://iop.harvard.edu.

A Bitter Divide

The November 2020 presidential election was one of the most divisive in decades. When all the votes were counted, Democrat Joe Biden was declared the winner. Biden had won with 81 million votes. Republican Donald Trump received 74 million votes. The Electoral College vote (306 for Biden, 232 for Trump) confirmed Biden's victory. While the official tallies gave Biden a clear victory, Trump and his supporters in government and the media repeatedly disputed the outcome of the election. In dozens of public statements and tweets, Trump claimed—without any evidence—that the election was rigged and stolen. More than three weeks after the election, Trump tweeted, "Biden can only enter the White House as President if he can prove that his ridiculous '80,000,000 votes' were not fraudulently or illegally obtained."[1]

The tweet was sent after a federal judge in Pennsylvania rejected Trump's claim that his defeat in the state was caused by widespread fraud. Trump and his team of lawyers would go on to lose another twenty-five lawsuits challenging the election results in courts across the country. These cases contested the manner in which the election was held, the way votes were counted, and the methods election officials used to certify vote totals.

Trump's claims of a stolen election, which critics—including Biden—dubbed "The Big Lie,"[2] were dismissed by the federal agency that oversees election security. A week after the election, the Cybersecurity and Infrastructure Security Agency released this statement: "The November 3rd election was the most secure in

5

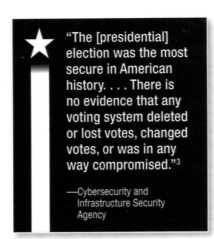
American history. . . . There is no evidence that any voting system deleted or lost votes, changed votes, or was in any way compromised."[3] This statement was backed by nonpartisan election officials in states where routine recounts were conducted, voting machines were inspected, and other measures were taken to ensure the election results were both fair and accurate.

Enacting New Election Laws

Certifiable facts seemed to hold little weight for millions of Americans who believed the election was stolen from Trump. A poll conducted by the Monmouth University Polling Institute in 2021 showed that 32 percent of all Americans—and 63 percent of Republicans—believed that Biden's victory was a result of massive election fraud. Although no evidence of widespread fraud has surfaced, this accusation has been kept alive by governors and members of Congress in states such as Texas, Georgia, Arizona, and Florida.

Based on these unsupported claims, in early 2021 lawmakers across the country began passing a raft of new voting restrictions. According to the nonpartisan Brennan Center for Justice, during January through September of that year, nineteen states passed thirty-one bills that tighten voting rules. Ninety percent of the laws were sponsored by Republican politicians. New voting laws increased voter ID requirements, reduced access to mail-in ballots, and cut the number of places voters could vote or drop off ballots. Some new election laws empower partisan poll watchers to record videos inside polling places, an invasive practice critics say can lead to voter intimidation.

In September 2021 Texas passed one of the nation's most restrictive new voting laws. The law begins with this statement: "Reforms are needed to the election laws of this state to ensure that fraud does not undermine the public confidence in the electoral process."[4] Texas Democratic lawmakers, all of whom opposed the bill, contend the law has nothing to do with voter fraud because there was no widespread fraud in the 2020 election. The new law, they say, has only one purpose: to make it harder for people to vote. Texas Democrat Chris Turner says, "This bill was never about election security or voter integrity. It was always about using the Big Lie to justify restricting access to the ballot box."[5]

The Demographic Shift

There is strident disagreement on the effect of more restrictive election laws. However, studies show that these types of laws make it more difficult for some citizens to vote. A 2020 study by Henry Brady, dean of the Goldman School of Public Policy at the University of California, Berkeley, revealed that voter ID laws prevented an estimated 20 million Americans from casting ballots

People in Nevada line up to vote on Election Day, 2020. The US voting process is regulated by numerous laws intended to prevent fraud; however, voting restrictions can also make it more difficult for some people to vote.

in 2016. Most of the people who lacked the necessary identification, Brady says, were people of color, the young, the elderly, and low-income voters. These groups are less likely to have a driver's license or, in some cases, a license with a current address.

Opponents point to data released by the US Census Bureau in 2021 to explain efforts to pass new voting laws. The majority of Republican voters are older, White people without college degrees who live in rural areas. According to the US Census Bureau, this demographic made up only 40 percent of voters in 2020, down from over 50 percent in 2010. At the same time, the number of Black, Hispanic, and Asian Americans has increased. These demographic groups tend to be younger and are more likely to vote for Democrats. According to the 2020 census, people of color represent 43 percent of the country, up from 34 percent in 2010. The demographic shift is particularly notable in states such as Texas, Arizona, and Georgia, where Republicans are enacting the toughest new voting restrictions. Demographer William Frey states: "[Republicans] see the wave of demography coming and they are just trying to hold up a wall and keep it from smashing them in. It's the last bastion of their dominance, and they are doing everything they can."[6]

Most Want Fewer Restrictions

Despite the rush for new election laws, polls show that such changes are not supported by a majority of Americans. According to a 2021 Monmouth poll, most Americans, regardless of political affiliation, feel that new restrictions on voting are not needed. A large majority, 71 percent, believe in-person voting should be easy; about half say voting by mail should also be easy. Around two-thirds of Americans support the idea of having a unified set of rules for voting in all fifty states (as opposed to the state-by-state system that currently exists). But voters still support strict ID laws; 80 percent said people should be required to show an ID when they vote. Patrick Murphy, director of the Monmouth University Polling Institute, sums up the results: "The poll contains some seemingly conflicting information on voter access. The bottom line seems to be that most Democrats and Republicans want to take the potential for election results to be questioned off the table. The problem, though, is they aren't likely to agree on how to get there."[7] As long as Americans remain sharply divided politically, battles over voting rights and voter suppression will dominate headlines.

CHAPTER ONE

Voting Rights in the United States

Throughout American history, millions of people have been shut out of the voting process. When the US Constitution was enacted in 1783, the vote was only available to White, male property owners. Most states began allowing White men who did not own property to vote during the 1840s. Black men could not vote until 1870, when they were granted voting rights by the Fifteenth Amendment to the Constitution: "The right of citizens of the United States to vote shall not be denied or abridged by the United States or by any State on account of race, color, or previous condition of servitude." Despite this guarantee of voting rights, Black Americans were restricted by onerous laws that prevented them from voting in southern states for nearly a century. Women, who began fighting for voting rights in the 1850s, could not vote until 1920, when the Nineteenth Amendment was added to the Constitution. Native Americans could not vote in most states until 1924.

The ability to cast a ballot is one of the most hard-won rights in American history. But in 2020 only about two-thirds of the voting-eligible population voted in the presidential election. And this was the highest percentage in at least sixty years. Voter participation was greater than usual because of a unique set of circumstances surrounding the election. According to the Pew Research Center, 83 percent of Americans said it really mattered who won in the bitter fight between Trump and Biden. Another factor was the COVID-19 pandemic, which was killing thousands of people every day around the time of the November election. Most states sent mail-in ballots to all registered voters to reduce face-to-face contact at the polls. This made it much easier for people to cast a ballot and undoubtedly helped increase voter participation.

Even with the higher-than-usual turnout in 2020, one-third of the electorate, or around 80 million Americans, did not vote. And the number of nonvoters in midterm elections, held between presidential elections, is usually much higher. In the 2018 midterms only around half of voting-age citizens cast a ballot. During the 2014 midterms voter turnout was a dismal 42 percent.

Millions of voters are apathetic; they dislike politics or believe their votes do not matter. Some are discouraged from voting in presidential elections because of the way presidents are picked through the Electoral College. This system, outlined in the Constitution, grants states the right to pick the president depending on the outcome of the popular vote in their state. In states that are dominated by one party, those in the opposing party have little reason to vote for a president since their votes will be outnumbered when it comes to choosing the president in the Electoral College.

Factors other than apathy help drive down voter turnout. Since the early 2010s dozens of states have made it harder to vote. Florida, Tennessee, Kentucky, and other states cut off voter registration around one month before an election. Voters who do not plan ahead by registering to vote cannot cast a ballot on Election Day. At least thirty-three states have voter identification requirements that shut out voters who lack a driver's license or other form of official ID. Some states also have complex bureaucratic processes that make voting by mail difficult. According to researcher Sean McElwee at the voting reform think tank Demos, "This new generation of election policies and rules are targeted at certain groups and disproportionately affect people of color, people who are poor, and young people."[8]

"This new generation of election policies and rules are targeted at certain groups and disproportionately affect people of color, people who are poor, and young people."[8]

—Sean McElwee, voting reform researcher

States Make the Rules

Voting rights remain a contentious issue in the twenty-first century because of the way the US Constitution was written in the 1780s. The elections clause in the Constitution empowers the states to determine the "Times, Places, And Manner" of elections. This means there are no centralized rules that govern elections for the entire country. Legislators in each state decide how people register to vote, how votes are counted, how fraud is prevented, and other issues that govern voting processes. This means that voting can be very easy in one state and very difficult in another. This is not the case in most democracies, where one set of rules governs all elections within that country. For example, German voters follow the same election rules in the state of Bavaria as they do in the state of Saxony.

The election powers granted to state legislators were responsible for one of the longest-running battles over voting rights in US history. In the decades after the Civil War, states in the South

In the 2020 election, most states sent voters mail-in ballots that they could complete at home and drop in a mailbox. This made it easier to vote and is believed to have increased voter participation.

The Electoral College

In the twenty-first century, two men were elected president after losing the popular vote: George W. Bush in 2000 and Donald Trump in 2016. This was due to a feature of American democracy called the Electoral College. This system for picking a president and vice president was established in the Constitution.

When voters go to the polls every four years to elect a president, they are not technically voting for the candidate of their choice. They are voting for a slate of delegates, called electors, who represent their state in the Electoral College. After the election, the electors cast their votes for the candidate who won the popular vote in their state. Although presidential candidate Hillary Clinton received 2.8 million more votes than Trump in 2016, she won the popular vote in fewer states. When all the electoral votes were counted, Trump received 306 while Clinton received 238.

Many Americans think the Electoral College is archaic, antidemocratic, and outdated. In a 2021 Pew Research Center poll, 55 percent of Americans surveyed said that the winner of the popular vote nationwide should win the presidency. Only 43 percent supported the Electoral College.

passed dozens of laws to prevent Black Americans from voting. Since the right to vote is called the franchise, the effect of these laws is referred to as disenfranchisement. The voting struggle of civil rights activist Fannie Lou Hamer is perhaps one of the best-known examples of Black disenfranchisement.

In the early 1960s Hamer lived and worked on a plantation in Sunflower County, Mississippi. At the time Black people made up 65 percent of the population in Mississippi, but only 2 percent were registered to vote. Whites, who made up 33 percent of the state, held all political offices. White people in Mississippi and other states throughout the South held on to power through state laws that made it nearly impossible for Black people to vote.

When Hamer tried to register to vote in Indianola, Mississippi, in 1962, she had to fill out a registration document, officially called a literacy test, which contained twenty-one questions. Literacy tests were only given to Black citizens who tried to register to vote. Small errors in filling out the form, such as missing a comma in the date, would lead to immediate disqualification. When Hamer tried to register, one of the questions on the literacy test required her to write a paragraph explaining the meaning of complex regulations in the Mississippi state constitution. Hamer could not provide a response that was satisfactory to the county clerk, and she was not allowed to register to vote.

The day after Hamer attempted to practice her constitutional right to register to vote, she was fired from her job. She was also evicted from the plantation where she had lived for eighteen years. Undaunted, Hamer studied the state constitution and passed the literacy test in January 1963. But when she tried to vote in the primary election the following March, she could not cast a ballot. She was told she had failed to pay what was called a poll tax. The Mississippi poll tax was two dollars, equal to around twenty dollars in 2021. Hamer paid the poll tax and voted. She went on to become one of the leading voting rights activists of the 1960s. But on various occasions Hamer was arrested, severely beaten, and shot at for trying to exercise her voting rights.

Passing the Civil Rights Act

Literacy tests and poll taxes were enforced in Alabama, Georgia, Louisiana, South Carolina, Virginia, and elsewhere. In some states, like Louisiana, the literacy tests contained confusing, convoluted questions that were impossible to answer. The late civil rights activist and former US representative John Lewis once described the onerous test administered by county clerks in his home state of Alabama:

> [The literacy test] was a sixty-eight-question survey about obscure aspects of state and federal regulation. Citizens might be asked to recite verbatim long portions of the U.S. Constitution. Some were even asked irrelevant questions such as the number of bubbles in a bar of soap. Black people with Ph.D. and M.A. degrees were routinely told they did not read well enough to pass the test.[9]

Fannie Lou Hamer, pictured here in 1964, was arrested, beaten, and shot at for trying to exercise her voting rights in Mississippi during the 1960s.

Many of those who overcame ballot box barriers had to then face violence from racist organizations, including White Citizens' Councils and the Ku Klux Klan. As Lewis wrote in 2005, "People who tried to register to vote or who encouraged black citizens to register were arrested, jailed, beaten, and killed. Some were fired from their jobs, separated from their families, evicted from their homes, and threatened with the loss of everything they had."[10]

The issue of voter suppression in the South made national headlines for years before the government finally acted. Congress passed the Voting Rights Act of 1965

"People who tried to register to vote or who encouraged black citizens to register were arrested, jailed, beaten, and killed."[10]

—John Lewis, civil rights activist

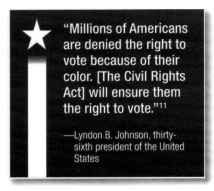

on August 6 of that year. At the signing ceremony, President Lyndon B. Johnson made clear that supporting the act was a moral duty for all Americans: "This act flows from a clear and simple wrong. Its only purpose is to right that wrong. Millions of Americans are denied the right to vote because of their color. This law will ensure them the right to vote. The wrong is one which no American, in his heart, can justify. The right is one which no American, true to our principles, can deny."[11]

The Voting Rights Act reinforced the language of the Fifteenth Amendment, which prohibited any practice that might deny or abridge the right to vote because of a person's race. Another general provision in the law forbade the use of poll taxes and literacy tests. Anyone who attempted to interfere with the right to vote could face civil and criminal penalties.

Special Provisions

The Voting Rights Act contains special provisions. A provision called Section 4 was written because voter discrimination was more prevalent in southern states and certain counties located in four other states. All areas covered by Section 4—states and counties—are referred to as jurisdictions. Section 4 created what is called a coverage formula, based on voting data, to determine where voter restrictions were in place as of November 1964. The jurisdictions in the coverage formula included Alabama, Alaska, Georgia, Louisiana, Mississippi, South Carolina, Texas, and Virginia. The coverage formula also singled out counties in Arizona, Hawaii, Idaho, and North Carolina where voting rights were denied to various groups, including Hispanics, Native Americans, Pacific Islanders, and African Americans.

Congress amended Section 4 of the Voting Rights Act several times after its initial passage. One significant change was enacted in 1975, when the law was expanded to cover so-called language minorities, which Congress defined as Native Americans, Alaska Natives, and people of Asian and Hispanic descent. Lawmakers felt these voters needed extra protection at a time when states like Arizona and Texas were only printing ballots in English.

A second provision of the Voting Rights Act, Section 5, required that jurisdictions named in Section 4 obtain federal permission before making any changes in their voting laws. Permission could be granted by the state's attorney general or by a three-judge panel on the district court in Washington, DC. Under Section 5, the jurisdictions were required to prove that proposed voting changes would not negatively impact any individual's right to vote based on race or minority status.

The Section 5 process is called preclearance. Officials must preapprove, or clear, minor changes to voting procedures, like

The Right to Vote Amendment

Some critics of voting laws in the United States would like to add the Right to Vote Amendment to the Constitution. The amendment, introduced in the US House of Representatives by Wisconsin representative Mark Pocan in 2018, states, "Every citizen of the United States, who is of legal voting age, shall have the fundamental right to vote in any public election held in the jurisdiction in which the citizen resides." Supporters say a constitutional amendment would abolish state laws that restrict the fundamental right to vote while overriding recent Supreme Court decisions that weakened the Voting Rights Act. Opponents do not believe the proposed amendment is necessary as there are already laws in place that protect voter rights.

Regardless of one's position on this amendment, all agree that passage is unlikely. The Constitution has only been amended seventeen times since 1791. Proposed new amendments must pass both houses of Congress by a two-thirds majority. Then amendments have to be ratified, or approved, by three-fourths of state legislatures. Given the hostility and polarized politics of the moment, that is unlikely to happen.

Mark Pocan, "H.J.Res.74—Proposing an Amendment to the Constitution of the United States Regarding the Right to Vote," Congress.gov, March 9, 2017. www.congress.gov.

moving a polling place. Preclearance was also required for major changes, such as requiring voters to present certain types of identification. In a 2005 essay, Lewis explained how Section 5 works: "The federal government essentially has the power to stop discriminatory voting changes before they are enacted into law. Therefore, Section 5 serves as a significant deterrent to the advancement of discriminatory legislation, making jurisdictions seriously consider the impact of changes they propose."[12]

Weakening the Voting Rights Act

In the decades after the Civil Rights Act was passed, polls consistently showed that around three-quarters of Americans approved of the law. However, opponents challenged the act in court twenty-one times between 1966 and 2009. During this period the Supreme Court consistently ruled that the Civil Rights Act was necessary to enforce the voting rights guaranteed by the Constitution. However, Section 5 of the Voting Rights Act was not permanent; Congress was required to renew it periodically. In 2006 Congress held hearings that highlighted the persistence of racial discrimination during elections. Congress heard reports of polling places in Black and Hispanic neighborhoods being moved in Texas, without notice, days before an election. They heard about aggressive poll watchers in Arkansas who demanded identification from Black voters and illegally watched as they filled out their ballots. And in Alabama English-only policies resulted in Spanish-speaking citizens who were not fluent in English shying away from voting. After the hearings, politicians in both parties voted overwhelmingly (390 to 33) to extend the preclearance requirement for another twenty-five years.

In 2010 officials in Shelby County, Alabama, which was 90 percent white at the time, decided to challenge the Voting Rights Act in court. Shelby County attorney Frank "Butch" Ellis believed the law was an expensive burden; the county did not want to spend taxpayer dollars to obtain preclearance for minor changes

President Lyndon Johnson meets with civil rights activists on the day that he signed the 1965 Voting Rights Act. The act prohibits any practices that infringe on the right to vote based on a person's race.

such as moving a polling station across the street. He filed a lawsuit against US attorney general Eric Holder, a case referred to as *Shelby County v. Holder*. Ellis argued that Sections 4 and 5 of the Voting Rights Act were unconstitutional. In June 2013 the Supreme Court struck down Section 4 of the Voting Rights Act. Although Section 5 was not ruled unconstitutional, the provision is meaningless without the coverage formula provided by Section 4. Lewis reacted to the judgment: "Today the Supreme Court stuck a dagger in the heart of the Voting Rights Act of 1965."[13]

Tightening Voting Rules

The effects of the Supreme Court ruling were immediate. Within hours, Texas implemented a strict voter ID law that had been blocked by the US Department of Justice in 2012 on the grounds that it was discriminatory. The Texas law compelled voters, when casting a ballot, to present a driver's license, passport, military ID, or concealed-gun permit. In what critics viewed as a move to disenfranchise young people of voting age, student ID cards were not accepted. Proponents of voter ID laws say they guard against voter fraud. However, the nonpartisan voting advocacy group Brennan Center for Justice says that more than six hundred thousand Texas voters lacked the identification needed to vote. Most of them were Black, Hispanic, young, or elderly.

By 2015 eight of the nine states previously requiring preclearance had passed new voting laws. While the US Department of Justice had previously stopped such restrictions from being implemented, it would now be left up to individuals to challenge the laws in court. To do so, challengers, called plaintiffs, would be required to prove that the voting law caused them personal harm. This standard is very difficult to prove in court. Additionally, plaintiffs who wished to challenge any new election law would be required to pay for lawyers and other legal expenses. In the past, US Department of Justice lawyers handled such cases.

The 2013 Supreme Court ruling was criticized by many people, including the nation's first Black president. As Barack Obama wrote after the decision, "For nearly 50 years, the Voting Rights Act . . . has helped secure the right to vote for millions of Americans. Today's decision invalidating one of its core provisions upsets decades of well-established practices that help make sure voting is fair, especially in places where voting discrimination has been historically prevalent."[14] Though much has changed since Fannie Lou Hamer tried to register in 1962, some citizens are still fighting for their right to vote.

CHAPTER TWO

Ballot Barriers

The year was 1883. The city was Chicago. Politicians who were fearful of losing elections, and thus their power, enacted new, more stringent voting laws. The new laws severely reduced opportunities for registration, allowing voters to register only on a few specified days. Additionally, a list purporting to contain the names of people who had registered improperly was created. Supporters justified these changes by claiming that widespread voter fraud was threatening election integrity. Voting officials hired investigators to search for evidence of voter fraud at polling places. They offered a reward to anyone who provided authorities with information leading to the arrest and conviction of someone who cast an illegal vote. The search for election fraud proved futile; no one found evidence of fraud at polling places.

Politicians have been drumming up unwarranted fears of voter fraud for as long as democratic elections have been held in the United States. According to Harvard University historian Alexander Keyssar, false claims of election fraud go back to the mid-1800s: "Legislative debates were sprinkled heavily with tales of ballot box stuffing, miscounts, hordes of immigrants lined up to vote as . . . instructed, men trooping from precinct to precinct to vote early and often."[15]

Similar allegations were made to attendees of Turning Point USA's Teen Student Action Summit in 2019 by President Donald Trump. "Those illegals get out and vote," he said. "They've got people voting that shouldn't be voting. They vote many times, not just twice, not just three times. It's like a circle. They come

back, they put a new hat on. They come back, they put a new shirt on. . . . It's a rigged deal."[16] Much like in the 1880s, proof of voter fraud as described by the president never materialized.

In fact, voter fraud does occasionally happen, but experts say it is rare. Justin Levitt, a voting expert and law professor, has studied more than 1.5 billion ballots cast in national elections since 2000 and found just 45 instances of fraud. "It doesn't happen often at all," says Levitt. "But when it happens it's a one-off: One person decides to file a false ballot or something like that."[17] Levitt's study has been backed up by other nonpartisan researchers at Columbia University, Arizona State University, and the US Government Accountability Office. Additionally, a 2017 study by the Brennan Center for Justice showed the rate of voting fraud in the United States to be less than 0.0009 percent.

Such was the case in Florida, where three individuals were charged with casting more than one ballot in the 2020 election. Florida voting records showed that two of the three were registered Republicans; the third person had no party affiliation. All three had voted in Florida and used absentee ballots from other states to cast a second ballot. The charge of casting more than one ballot in an election, is a third-degree felony that carries a penalty of up to five years in prison.

Absentee Voting

While illegal voting is extremely rare, claims of voter fraud were at a fever pitch during the run-up to the 2020 election. Much of the controversy centered on absentee ballots, often referred to as mail-in ballots or vote by mail. These ballots are so named because they are provided to voters who expect to be absent from, or unable to visit, their local polling places on Election Day. Traditionally, this has included military personnel serving overseas, US citizens who live and work in other countries, people who planned to be on vacation or attending an out-of-town business meeting on Election Day, or people with disabilities who have difficulty voting in person.

The rules for voting with absentee ballots vary from state to state. In 2000 Oregon became the first state to automatically mail absentee ballots to all voters in every election. Before the 2020 election four other states were also conducting elections entirely by mail—Colorado, Hawaii, Utah, and Washington. (California joined this group in 2021.) In 2020 thirty-four states had what is called no-excuse absentee voting. With no-excuse absentee voting, any voter can request an absentee ballot without providing a reason. In Texas no-excuse absentee voting is only available to voters age sixty-five and older. Other states require voters to offer a reason as to why they cannot visit their polling place on Election Day. These states also require voters to provide a photocopy of their driver's license or other official ID when requesting an absentee ballot.

Voting in the United States is subject to strict oversight, and despite frequent accusations of voter fraud, fraud is actually rare. Here, election workers in Florida load ballots into the vote counting machine on Election Day 2020.

Elections experts consider absentee ballots safer than the outdated electronic voting machines found in many polling places. While machines can break down or be hacked, absentee ballots provide a paper record of a voter's choices. This ballot can be inspected for fraud and counted—and recounted—after the polls close. And according to a 2020 Pew Research Center poll, two-thirds of voters support no-excuse absentee voting because casting a ballot at home and dropping it in a ballot box or mailbox is easier than visiting a polling place and standing in line to vote.

Claims of Fraud

Before 2020, absentee ballots were rarely seen as controversial. In 2016 nearly 139 million people voted in the presidential election. Around 21 percent, or 29 million votes, were cast with absentee ballots. But there was a major expansion in mail voting in 2020 due to the COVID-19 pandemic. In an effort to slow the spread of the disease by eliminating in-person voting, officials in forty-four states sent all registered voters absentee ballots. This change sparked a national debate after Trump began attacking absentee ballots. According to a *Washington Post* database of his tweets, speeches, and written statements, Trump made more than 150 untruthful claims about absentee ballots during April through November 2020 alone. Without proof, he claimed that voting by mail was a dangerous scam, unconstitutional, and rife with fraud. The reason for these attacks came to light on the talk show *Fox & Friends* in March 2020 when Trump said if the United States switched to all-mail voting, "you'd never have a Republican elected in this country again."[18] Trump's claims were proved wrong. While he lost the presidential election, Republicans picked up fifteen seats in the House of Representatives and remained in control of most states where they were already in power.

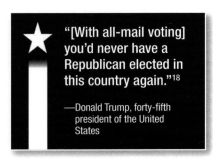

"[With all-mail voting] you'd never have a Republican elected in this country again."[18]

—Donald Trump, forty-fifth president of the United States

After the election, the statistics website FiveThirtyEight analyzed the role of

The Arizona Search for Voter Fraud

Joe Biden won the popular vote in Arizona in 2020, a result confirmed by a hand recount of all ballots. However, without evidence, Donald Trump claimed that there was widespread voter fraud in the state. In April 2021 Trump's charges prompted the Republican-led Arizona state senate to hire a security company called Cyber Ninjas to conduct an election audit. Cyber Ninjas had no experience in election recounts, and its chief executive officer was a Trump supporter who promoted wild conspiracy theories about election fraud.

Observers were shocked by the unscientific, sometimes bizarre, methods Cyber Ninjas used to recount 2.21 million Arizona ballots. Workers used microscopes to search for bamboo fibers in ballots, based on the outlandish rumor that claimed forty thousand Biden ballots were smuggled in from Asia. When the haphazard audit was concluded in September, Biden actually picked up an extra ninety-nine votes. Journalist Philip Bump called the Arizona audit dangerous: "[Cyber Ninjas was] hired to slather some semblance of authority on top of conspiracy theories. To anchor irrational assumptions about fraud to something resembling rationality."

Philip Bump, "The Arizona Election Review Did Exactly What It Was Intended to Do," *Washington Post*, September 24, 2021. www.washingtonpost.com.

absentee ballots in the 2020 election. The site found that allowing all registered voters to cast ballots by mail helped increase turnout. A record 160 million people voted in the presidential election, and more than 73 million of those votes were absentee ballots, another record. In some states the increase in mail voting was astonishing. For example, in New Jersey only 7 percent of the votes in 2016 were absentee ballots. In 2020 that number was 86 percent. By contrast, states that required voters to provide a non–pandemic related excuse to receive an absentee ballot showed little change. In one such state, Texas, the rate of mail voting in 2020 was 11 percent, barely up from the 7 percent of 2016.

In addition to increasing the number of people voting by mail, absentee ballots changed the 2020 election in another way. According to FiveThirtyEight, the majority of votes cast by mail favored Biden, while Trump won votes cast in person in polling places on Election Day. With more people than ever voting by mail, Biden's victory was assured. Election analysts Nathaniel

Rakich and Jasmine Mithani explain why this mattered: "It's not hard to see why Trump, then, in his desperation to hold onto power, claimed that Democrats used mail ballots to steal the election from him. Biden indeed would not have won without mail votes, but there is no evidence that a significant number of these votes were cast fraudulently."[19]

Despite the lack of evidence, Trump spent millions of dollars to contest the results of the election. He hired lawyers to file numerous lawsuits that focused on absentee ballots in states won by Biden, including Georgia, Michigan, and Wisconsin. In Pennsylvania Trump relentlessly repeated false claims about widespread voter fraud. This rhetoric was the basis of a lawsuit in which Trump's lawyers tried to convince a federal judge to disqualify all 2.5 million absentee ballots cast in the Pennsylvania election. The failed lawsuit would have nullified the voting rights of enough

As a result of the COVID-19 pandemic, there was a surge in the use of absentee ballots in the 2020 election. Former president Donald Trump falsely claimed, as in this Facebook post, that increased mail voting would cause widespread fraud.

m.facebook.com/Do

Donald J. Trump ✔
17 hrs · 🌐

Mail-In Voting, unless changed by the courts, will lead to the most CORRUPT ELECTION in our Nation's History! #RIGGEDELECTION

Get official voting info on how to vo the 2020 US Election at usa.gov.

ⓘ ...et Voting Information

people to throw the state's twenty electoral votes to Trump. District Court judge Matthew Brann wrote the court order against Trump in the case. Referring to baseless claims of voter fraud, the judge wrote: "In the United States of America, this cannot justify the disenfranchisement of a single voter, let alone all the voters of its sixth most populated state."[20] Trump's lawyers appealed the ruling to the US Supreme Court, which refused to hear the case.

Florida Tightens Ballot Rules

While no state or federal judges found problems with absentee ballots, after Trump's loss, Republicans in at least eighteen states passed new laws targeting this popular method of voting. Florida was one of the first to act. In the 2020 election 2.2 million of the state's absentee ballots came from Democrats; 1.5 million came from Republicans. This was a switch from previous years, when more Republicans than Democrats voted by mail. On the one hand, Florida's Republican governor, Ron DeSantis, acknowledged that the 2020 election in his state was conducted in a smooth and successful manner. On the other hand, he supported a new law, called SB 90, that places limits on voting by mail.

That law, passed by state legislators in 2021, requires Florida voters to reapply for an absentee ballot every two-year election cycle, rather than every four years. It also limits where the ballots can be delivered. In 2020 around 1.5 million Florida voters deposited their absentee ballots in drop boxes that were open twenty-four hours a day. While drop boxes are usually available for about two weeks before the election, large counties put them to use earlier due to the pandemic. Under the new law, drop boxes will only be available on early voting days and not on Election Day.

SB 90 requires drop boxes to be supervised by election officials at all times. Before the law was passed, some counties relied on video surveillance to keep drop boxes secure. In Palm Beach County in 2020, some drop boxes were supervised by

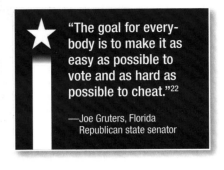

sheriff's office employees. The new provision restricts the availability of drop boxes to hours when election officials are on duty, typically from 7:00 a.m. to 7:00 p.m. Drop boxes will not be available to voters at night. Election officials who fail to comply with the new drop box rules can be fined $25,000.

New York Times reporter Adeel Hassan says drop box restrictions are aimed at Black and Hispanic voters: "Voters of color are most reliant on after-hours drop boxes . . . as it's often more difficult for them to both take hours off during the day and to organize transportation to polling places."[21]

Republican state senator Joe Gruters explains why SB 90 was needed: "The goal for everybody is to make it as easy as possible to vote and as hard as possible to cheat."[22] But neither Gruters nor any other Florida officials provided evidence of election fraud in their state to demonstrate the need for stricter laws. According to one unnamed Republican member of the Florida board of elections supervisors, "[SB 90 is] stupid, OK? It was a solution looking for a problem."[23]

Bills Written by a Think Tank

The language of the Florida election law is similar to measures that were passed in 2021 in Arizona, Georgia, Iowa, Texas, and elsewhere. These laws sound similar because they were written and promoted by the Heritage Foundation, a conservative think tank that spent $24 million in 2021 on efforts to pass a new round of restrictive voting laws. As Heritage Foundation executive director Jessica Anderson told donors at a 2021 fund-raiser, "We're working with state legislators to ensure they have all the information they need to draft the [election] bills. In some cases we actually draft [the bills] for them."[24]

The Heritage Foundation has been pushing for tighter voter restrictions since its founding in 1973. Cofounder Paul Weyrich was clear about the group's aims in a 1980 speech to evangelical

A number of states recently tightened ballot rules. Critics such as voting rights activist Stacey Abrams (pictured) worry that these restrictions will make it more difficult for people of color to vote in future elections.

leaders: "I don't want everybody to vote. Elections are not won by a majority of the people. They never have been from the beginning of our country and they are not now. As a matter of fact, our leverage in the elections quite candidly goes up as the voting populace goes down."[25]

A Changing Electorate

Statistics compiled by the Brennan Center suggest why groups like the Heritage Foundation are working to toughen ballot rules. In past elections, mail-in ballots were used mostly by White voters. In 2016, for instance, 67 percent of all mail voters nationwide were White, compared to 54 percent in 2020. During those same years, the number of Black voters using absentee ballots increased from 23 percent to 31 percent. In Texas, during the 2020 election, 56 percent of absentee ballots deposited in twenty-four-hour drop boxes were from people of color, according to the voting rights group Texas Rising. Due to the state's new restrictions, these boxes will not be available in 2022.

Black voting rights activist and former Georgia legislator Stacey Abrams believes that recent voting laws, especially those that impose barriers on balloting, are intended to make voting more difficult for some. "These are laws that respond to an increase in voting by people of color by constricting, removing or otherwise harming their ability to access [the ballot box]. It doesn't say brown and Black people can't vote. It simply says we're going to remove things that we saw you use to your benefit; we're going to make it harder for you to access these opportunities."[26]

While the new election restrictions in Florida, Georgia, and Texas produced the most headlines in 2021, laws that affect the voting rights for millions of people have passed in other states. In Arkansas, absentee ballots must be received four days before Election Day, making the state one of two where absentee ballots that arrive on Election Day do not count. In Indiana, drop boxes must be controlled and supervised by the county election board at all times. This is meant to reduce the hours when drop boxes can be used.

Who Benefits from Mail Voting?

During and after the 2020 election, Republican politicians nationwide have characterized absentee voting as rife with the potential for fraud. This represents a big change from earlier elections when Republican lawmakers touted the benefits of absentee voting. In 2002, for example, Florida Republicans enacted a no-excuse vote-by-mail system. At the time, several prominent Republican politicians in Florida, including Governor Jeb Bush, believed mail voting helped them win tight elections. This prompted Florida Republicans to pass a law a few years later that allowed voters to automatically receive absentee ballots for four years. The laws seemed to work to Republican advantage; the party has largely controlled state government for more than twenty years.

When Donald Trump began attacking mail voting in 2020, Florida politicians reversed themselves and enacted restrictions aimed at absentee ballots. This has caused many Republicans to fear that the new laws will hurt their chances in the future.

As Abrams makes clear, the new laws do not prevent people from voting, they just make it much more inconvenient. And the laws have not been in force long enough to show how they will affect elections, since voters in both political parties will be subject to the new restrictions. What the restrictions have done is mobilize activists who oppose them. For example, Black volunteers in Georgia were going door-to-door in 2021, a year ahead of the midterm elections, to register voters while ensuring people of color had the proper information they needed to cast ballots. As volunteer Tammye Pettyjohn Jones says, "You don't have time to hem and haw about how hard it is [to vote]. . . . You've got to go into a problem-solving mode."[27] As recent elections show, political outcomes are unpredictable. While some might hope to improve their chances by instituting new laws, others will work harder to ensure their votes are counted in every election.

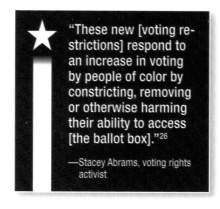

"These new [voting restrictions] respond to an increase in voting by people of color by constricting, removing or otherwise harming their ability to access [the ballot box]."[26]

—Stacey Abrams, voting rights activist

CHAPTER THREE

Polling Place Pressures

Voting in the United States is a keystone of the democratic system of government. High voter turnout is a sign of an engaged population—and a healthy democracy. However, election laws are increasingly making voting more complicated and more difficult—which could lead to fewer eligible voters having their say.

Polling place practices vary from state to state—and they can be confusing. In some states a signature on a driver's license must exactly match the signature that was given at the time of voter registration. Some states drop people from voter rolls if they have not voted in previous elections. States might require specific forms of ID for voting—and reject others. Sometimes, even finding a polling place close to home is difficult. Other times the problem is not finding a place to vote but getting stuck in line for hours to cast a ballot. While many Americans navigate these processes, the rules make it more difficult for people to vote.

Many of these issues were in play during one of the most compelling elections of 2018, the Georgia governor's race between Democrat Stacey Abrams and Republican Brian Kemp. Abrams was the first Black woman in US history to run for governor on a major party ticket. At the time, Kemp, who is White, was Georgia's secretary of state.

Black Georgia resident James Baiye II was excited to cast his vote for Abrams at his neighborhood polling place, the Lucerne

Baptist Church. Baiye was not a frequent voter. He had not cast a ballot since Barack Obama ran for president in 2008. Ten years later when Baiye tried to vote for Abrams, he was turned away. Election officials told him that his name was not on the list of registered voters. If a person's name is not on that list, they cannot vote. What Baiye did not know at the time was that Secretary of State Kemp had eliminated, or purged, over 1million names from state voter rolls from 2012 to 2018. And Baiye's name was one of them.

The Purging of Voter Rolls

All states purge voter rolls. This task eliminates the names of voters who have died, moved away, or lost the right to vote because they are in prison. The policy is meant to ensure the integrity of the electoral process. By purging names, the state eliminates the possibility that cheaters might use the names of the dead to cast fraudulent votes. And removing names of voters who have moved and registered elsewhere prevents people from casting ballots in two separate locations.

According to an investigation by the *Atlanta Journal-Constitution*, Georgia had purged about 1 million voter names from its rolls for these reasons. But, the newspaper found, another 400,000 names had been removed from voter rolls for an entirely different reason. These individuals had not cast a ballot in recent elections. Although they were still legally eligible to vote, they had been subjected to what has been referred to as a use-it-or-lose-it voting policy.

Only nine states purge infrequent voters from their rolls. In addition to Georgia, this number includes Ohio, Pennsylvania, and West Virginia. In Georgia, use-it-or-lose-it applies to anyone who has not voted in two previous elections. Before names are removed, voters are sent a postcard notifying them that they must reregister or they will lose their ability to vote. If they do not respond to the postcard, their names are purged. Baiye said he had been away at college when he skipped voting and never received notification from the state. He later said he felt like he was caught in a "loophole" meant to discourage people like him from voting: "It's kind of mind blowing. You're basically saying if I don't use my right [to vote], you'll take my right away. That's utterly ridiculous."[28]

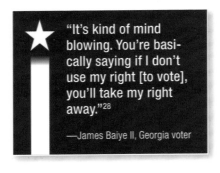

"It's kind of mind blowing. You're basically saying if I don't use my right [to vote], you'll take my right away."[28]

—James Baiye II, Georgia voter

Kemp had long emphasized the need to purge voter rolls to prevent fraud. In 2017, the same year he declared his intention to run for governor, Kemp set a national record—deleting 668,000 names in a single day. Kemp's office said 400,000 of those people had moved to another state. But investigative reporter Greg Palast later obtained the purge list and discovered that more than 340,000 people on that list had not moved out of state and were wrongly purged. Referring to the events of 2017, Palast says:

> Basically everyone [on the list] is what we call "purge by postcard" victims: They missed an election. They got a postcard to confirm their address. They didn't send back the postcard . . . they were cancelled without further notice on the grounds that that was evidence that they had moved. . . . You have to understand: One in ten Georgia voters were cancelled in a single year.[29]

In a three-month period before the November 2018 election, Kemp purged an additional eighty-five thousand names from voter rolls. The Associated Press studied the voting records of Georgia voters purged for nonvoting and found a racial disparity. While the state is 32 percent Black, more than 70 percent of purged voters were Black. Kemp defended his actions by saying: "We've had the same person voting twice in two different states in presidential elections. So there's a reason you keep the voter rolls

Purging voter rolls can make it more difficult for people to vote. Critics charge that Georgia's secretary of state, Brian Kemp (pictured voting in 2018), wrongly purged thousands of names from state rolls prior to the 2018 election.

current and up to date. We don't have near the problems other states have with voter fraud."[30]

Abrams lost the election to Kemp by around fifty-five thousand votes. After the election, Abrams said Kemp's massive purge of voter rolls amounted to "deliberate and intentional" voter suppression: "I acknowledge that former Secretary of State Brian Kemp will be certified as the victor in the 2018 gubernatorial election. But to watch an elected official who claims to represent the people in this state baldly pin his hopes for election on suppression of the people's democratic right to vote has been truly appalling."[31]

"There's a reason you keep the voter rolls current and up to date. We don't have near the problems other states have with voter fraud."[30]

—Brian Kemp, Georgia secretary of state

Making Voting Easier

While many states have been working to place barriers in front of the ballot box, California has implemented policies to make voting as easy and convenient as possible. California is a majority Democratic state where election officials have worked to reduce the wait time at the polls. Before each election, officials analyze election-related data, including the number of registered voters in each county, historic voter turnout, the capacity of each polling place, and even the number of available parking spots. Guided by this information, officials assign poll workers, distribute ballots, and direct voters to specific polling locations.

These efforts have drastically lowered wait times at California polls. According to Michael Scarpello, the registrar of voters for San Bernardino County, "If there are lines, they are short. At most, voters wait five minutes. . . . Our job is to make voting as convenient as possible for voters. If voters are motivated, we don't want to put any barriers in their way."

Quoted in Matt Vasilogambros, "Voting Lines Are Shorter—but Mostly for Whites," Huffington Post, February 15, 2018. www.huffingtonpost.com.

ID Hassles

New voter ID laws have also made it harder for people to vote. In 2020 thirty-five states required voters to show some form of ID at the polls. The laws are divided into two categories, strict and nonstrict. States with nonstrict laws, such as Colorado and Virginia, only require voters to sign a sworn affirmation that they are who they say they are. In strict states, including Arizona, Indiana, and Wisconsin, voters are required to possess a photo ID such as a state-issued driver's license, nondriver ID or voter card, US passport, or a military or tribal ID.

The most common form of ID is a driver's license, but millions of people do not drive because they cannot afford cars or do not require them because they live in urban areas where public transit is available. For these individuals, an official state ID card is often the next best option, but obtaining this form of ID usually requires one or more documents to prove one's identity. This includes out-of-state photo IDs, birth certificates, and marriage certificates—some or all of which are not always available.

Numerous academic studies show that the people least likely to have access to proper ID are racial and ethnic minorities, young adults, and people with disabilities.

Time and money are part of the problem. The paperwork to get an official ID costs money and requires citizens to take time to travel to the department of motor vehicles or other government office. According to the American Civil Liberties Union, the combined cost to obtain a government-issued ID ranges from $75 to $175 for document fees, travel expenses, and missed work. These requirements serve as a barrier to low-income voters seeking to secure an official ID.

Outlawing Drive-Through Voting

Voting in person can be difficult even for those who possess the proper ID. This was especially true in 2020 when the COVID-19 pandemic made it a possible health hazard to enter a polling place or wait in line to vote. As a way to make voting easier under these conditions, officials in Harris County, Texas, instituted a new process called drive-through early voting. This allowed voters to cast ballots on portable voting machines while remaining in their cars.

At a time when COVID-19 was infecting thousands of Texans every day, Harris County elections officials set up ten drive-through polling places under large tents. The option was popular; around 127,000 people used drive-through voting centers. More than half of those voters were Black, Latino, or Asian, according to Democratic state senator and Houston resident Carol Alvarado.

Drive-through voting was so successful that Harris County officials decided to use it in all future elections. But in 2021 a new Texas law banned the practice. Texas governor Greg Abbott argued in favor of the law, saying that drive-through voting might allow a driver to coerce his or her passengers to vote a certain way. Former Harris County election clerk Chris Hollins believes the reason for this drive-through voting ban can be found in the

Drive-through voting, shown here at a California polling place in 2020, became popular during the COVID-19 pandemic. It gave people a safer way to vote at a time when it was a possible health hazard to enter a polling location.

county's demographics. Harris County is home to Houston, the most populous city in Texas. Forty-four percent of the city's population is Hispanic, and 20 percent is Black—two groups that tend to vote for Democrats. Hollins believes this is why Texas Republicans outlawed drive-through voting: "The math is simple. Their take is, 'Let's make it harder for Harris County to vote.' Even though thousands of Republicans are going to be disenfranchised, too."[32]

Long Lines at Polling Places

Drive-through voting is not the only method of casting early ballots that has been targeted by politicians. In some states lawmakers have reduced early voting hours and severely cut the number of polling places. During early voting periods, voters can cast their ballots before Election Day at selected polling places. The process is meant to encourage voting and ease crowding. Fewer early voting days and fewer polling places have led to long lines for people wanting to vote.

This has happened in Georgia, where voter rolls grew by 2 million people from 2010 to 2020. During that same period Republican lawmakers cut the number of polling locations by 10 percent, according to an analysis of state voting records by ProPublica. Most of those cuts were in counties with large populations, especially Fulton and DeKalb counties where Atlanta is located. In Fulton County the average number of voters per polling place grew from about twenty-six hundred in 2012 to thirty-six hundred in 2020, an increase of 40 percent.

In the Atlanta suburb of Union City, which is 88 percent Black, some voters waited in line for hours to cast a ballot in the June 2020 primary election. Kathy, who did not want her last name used, was one such voter. She got in line to vote in Union City at 3:30 p.m. and did not get inside the polling place until after 8:00 p.m. By this time poll workers had already shut down voting machines. Workers gave Kathy a provisional ballot, a paper ballot provided to those who do not have proper ID or who experience other voting problems. The move upset Kathy, who was already stressed from waiting in line more than four hours. Speaking to a reporter after leaving her polling place, Kathy said, "I'm now angry again, I'm frustrated again, and now I have an added emotion, which is anxiety. I'm wondering if my ballot is going to count."[33]

Kathy's experience was not unique, and the problem carried over to the presidential election. On the first day of early voting in October 2020, dozens of Twitter videos from suburban Atlanta showed long lines of voters, many of whom waited six or more hours to vote. In one video, voter Johnta Austin said he waited in line eleven hours to cast a ballot. Another Atlanta voter, Steve Davidson, pointed out that his long wait was nothing compared to Black activists in the 1960s who were beaten and arrested to secure his right to vote: "They've been

> "I'm now angry again, I'm frustrated again, and now I have an added emotion, which is anxiety. I'm wondering if my ballot is going to count."[33]
>
> —Kathy, Georgia voter

fighting for decades. If I've got to wait six or seven hours, that's my duty to do that. I'll do it happily."[34]

Georgia is one of many states, mostly in the South, that have significantly cut the number of polling places in recent years. A 2019 report by the civil rights group Leadership Conference Education Fund found that 1,688 polling places had been closed in states that were formerly covered by Sections 4 and 5 of the Voting Rights Act. After the 2013 Supreme Court ruling that eliminated preclearance requirements, Louisiana closed 126 polling places; Mississippi, 96; Alabama, 72; and North Carolina, 72.

Texas leads the nation in the number of polling place closures; 750 polls have been closed since 2014. McLennan County, home to Waco, closed 44 percent of its polling places even as its population grew by more than fifteen thousand people. Brazoria County, south of Houston, lost nearly 60 percent of its voting locations. A study by the *Guardian* newspaper showed that the vast majority of these closures were in places with large numbers of Black and Hispanic voters.

Texas officials say that the polling place closures are the result of a 2014 state law that was supposed to make voting more convenient. The law created centralized countywide polling places called vote centers. Rather than have citizens vote at their local neighborhood polls, Texas voters could cast their ballots in any vote center in their county of residence. The centers were seen as a way to make voting easy, and they were originally supported by voting rights advocates and leaders of both political parties. But the law allowed any county that opened voting centers to close half of its neighborhood polling places. The problems with this plan were obvious on the first day of early voting in 2020, when the excessively long lines in Texas mirrored those in Georgia.

Intimidating Poll Workers

Contributing to the long waits was a shortage of election workers. In 2020 many election workers stayed away from the polls because of the COVID-19 pandemic. Election experts have warned

that fear is likely to be a factor in long wait times in future elections but not necessarily fear of COVID-19. Elections experts say intimidation could be a serious problem for reaching needed staffing levels at polling places. In the aftermath of the 2020 election, poll workers, many of whom are volunteers, were wrongly accused of throwing out ballots, purposely miscounting votes, and hacking voting machines to give Biden a victory. After the election, poll workers reported that they were followed by Trump supporters, photographed, and targeted with death threats.

The far-right website Gateway Pundit called two Black election workers in Georgia "traitors" and said they tried to "steal the presidential election in Georgia."[35] The women, who earned little more than fifteen dollars an hour, were targeted after Trump falsely named them as professional vote scammers. The phones

No Water or Food in Voting Lines

Voters in Atlanta and other parts of Georgia were forced to stand in long lines for hours at local polling places in 2020. In the future, while waiting to vote, they will also be prohibited from receiving food or drinks (including water) from volunteers. A provision of Georgia's Election Integrity Act of 2021 prohibits any person from passing out food or drinks to people waiting in line to vote. Anyone wishing to provide refreshments to voters on Election Day cannot be within 150 feet (46 m) of a polling place or within 25 feet (7.6 m) of any voter standing in line. Violations are punishable by one year in jail and a fine of up to $1,000. Supporters of the law view free food and water as potential bribes that might be provided by politicians and political organizations to influence voters. Joe Biden has characterized the law differently. He says, "[The Election Integrity Act] makes it a crime to provide water to voters while they wait in line—lines Republican officials themselves have created by reducing the number of polling sites across the state, disproportionately in Black neighborhoods."

Quoted in Tim Carman, "New Limits on Food and Water at Georgia's Polls Could Hinder Black and Low-Income Voters, Advocates Say," *Washington Post*, April 9, 2021. www.washingtonpost.com.

of the election workers were flooded with racial slurs and death threats, and people started banging on their doors late at night. All of this behavior forced them to change their appearance and go into hiding. The women, who sued Gateway Pundit in 2021, were among hundreds of elections workers and officials in fourteen states who received more than eight hundred threatening messages, according to Reuters.

Election officials are also being targeted by new state laws in Florida, Georgia, Texas, and elsewhere that levy large fines for technical violations. A 2021 bill passed in Florida carries a $25,000 penalty for election supervisors who fail to monitor a drop box in person. In Iowa election officials who commit minor errors like opening a polling place a few minutes late face fines of up to $10,000. The new penalties, coupled with the hostile atmosphere surrounding elections, has caused dozens of experienced officials to quit across the country. As president of the Wisconsin Municipal Clerks Association Wendy Helgeson says, "It's hard to convince someone it's a good way to give back to the community when you're afraid of going to . . . jail. It's harder and harder to get people to work in government."[36]

With fewer poll workers, long lines are expected to become the norm. And these lines prevent an unknown number of people from casting their ballots. But for all the controversy surrounding election issues, most Americans believe voting should be easier. According to a 2021 NPR/*PBS NewsHour*/Marist Poll, 56 percent of respondents say that states should be "making sure that everyone who wants to vote can do so."[37]

By sowing distrust, partisan politicians continue to suppress voter turnout and cause voters to question the legitimacy of the winning candidate. Whether those politicians will continue to remain in power is up to voters, who will have to overcome an increasing number of barriers to cast their ballots.

CHAPTER FOUR

Overcoming Legal Obstacles

Disagreements over voting rights and suppression often find their way into courtrooms. The US Supreme Court has the final say in such matters, but that does not usually end the debate. And sometimes Supreme Court rulings generate as much controversy as the cases themselves. This is what happened in July 2021 when the US Supreme Court issued a ruling in the case of *Brnovich v. Democratic National Committee*.

The case involved a practice that is common among the sixty-seven thousand Navajo voters who live on the sprawling Navajo Nation reservation in the Four Corners regions of northeastern Arizona. Many of the Navajo people living on this reservation are extremely poor and live in isolated dwellings that lack an official street address. According to voting rights attorney for the Native American Rights Fund Jacqueline De León, "People rely on P.O. boxes and they share P.O. boxes. I'm talking about like 10 to 15 people sharing a P.O. box."[38] This situation makes it difficult for residents to obtain a picture ID with a physical address, which is required in Arizona to register to vote, obtain an absentee ballot, and cast a ballot in person.

Some Navajo people do not own cars, and there is little public transportation on the reservation. This can be a problem during elections. Polling places and ballot drop boxes can be located anywhere from 20 to 100 miles (32 to 161 km) away from where voters live. And the unpaved reservation roads can be impassible due to harsh November weather when elections are held. This has long been a problem for people living on reservations, as De León says: "We saw time and time again that there were just unreasonable distances people had to travel in order to cast their vote."[39]

For many years Navajo voters managed to overcome the hurdles to the ballot box imposed by the rural nature of the reservation. People who lacked access to the polls could fill out absentee ballots and give them to a neighbor, tribal official, or voting rights activist to be delivered to the proper polling place. This practice, which is also common among Black and Hispanic voters, is known as ballot collection or ballot harvesting. Detractors say this process is ripe for fraud. They argue that political groups can coerce or threaten voters into voting a certain way or tamper with ballots after they are collected. Hans von Spakovsky of the Heritage Foundation explains his opposition to ballot collection: "Allowing individuals other than the voter or his immediate family to handle absentee ballots is a recipe for mischief and wrongdoing. . . . There is no guarantee that vote harvesters won't simply discard the ballots of voters whose political preferences for candidates of the opposition party are known."[40]

An Unequal Impact on Minority Voters

There have been very few instances of people cheating through ballot harvesting. But Republican politicians in Arizona cited voter fraud when they passed a law in 2016 that made ballot harvesting a felony. (The law exempts postal workers, family members, household members, and licensed caregivers who provide medical assistance.) Democrats in Arizona charged that the law targeted minority voters, and they filed a lawsuit challenging its legality. The law was put on hold until 2020, when the US Court of Appeals for the Ninth Circuit overturned the law. The court ruled that "criminalization of the collection of another person's ballot

[has] a discriminatory impact on American Indian, Hispanic, and African American voters in Arizona."[41]

The court of appeals ruled that the Arizona law violated Section 2 of the Voting Rights Act of 1965. Section 2 prohibits voting practices that result in citizens being denied equal access to the political process on account of race or membership in a language minority group.

Voting rights advocates celebrated the victory, but their joy was temporary. Arizona attorney general Mark Brnovich appealed the ruling to the Supreme Court. In their ruling, a majority of the justices sided with Arizona, which allowed the ballot harvesting law to go into effect. Supreme Court justice Samuel Alito wrote the majority opinion that ruled states can enact laws to prevent voter fraud, even if no voter fraud has been detected. Alito acknowledged that Arizona's ballot harvesting regulation makes it harder for people of color to vote. But he ruled that a law that makes voting inconvenient is not the same as a law that openly denies someone the right to vote. The burden imposed by the law, Alito

Many homes in the Navajo Nation are extremely isolated, lacking an official street address. This can make it hard for Navajo residents to register to vote.

wrote, was too modest to be in violation of the Voting Rights Act. Alito wrote, "Differences in employment, wealth, and education may make it virtually impossible for a state to devise rules that do not have some [unequal] impact"[42] on minority voters.

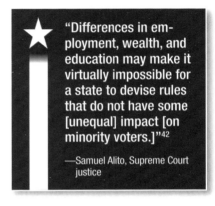

"Differences in employment, wealth, and education may make it virtually impossible for a state to devise rules that do not have some [unequal] impact [on minority voters.]"[42]

—Samuel Alito, Supreme Court justice

Supreme Court justice Elena Kagan disagreed with the majority opinion, writing a forty-one-page dissent that accused the court of deliberately undermining the Voting Rights Act: "What is tragic here is that the Court has rewritten—in order to weaken—[the Voting Rights Act] that stands as a monument to America's greatness, and protects against its basest impulses. What is tragic is that the Court has damaged a statute designed to bring about 'the end of discrimination in voting.'"[43]

John Lewis Voting Rights Act

Critics warn that the *Brnovich* ruling empowers politicians to write additional restrictive laws that will make voting harder for many citizens. The solution, they say, is for Congress to pass legislation that will protect every American's right to vote.

In 2021 the US House of Representatives took the first step toward doing that. The House passed the John Lewis Voting Rights Advancement Act, named after the late Georgia representative and civil rights activist John Lewis. The law would restore the preclearance requirement in Section 5 of the Voting Rights Act that was struck down by the Supreme Court in 2013. This means that states with a history of voter discrimination would once again have to get preapproval from the US Department of Justice before changing election laws. If passed, the Lewis act would block

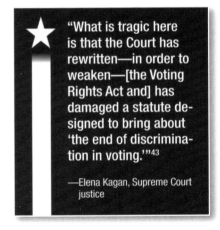

"What is tragic here is that the Court has rewritten—in order to weaken—[the Voting Rights Act and] has damaged a statute designed to bring about 'the end of discrimination in voting.'"[43]

—Elena Kagan, Supreme Court justice

"The John Lewis Voting Rights Advancement Act would help identify barriers that could silence Black, Latino, Indigenous, young and new Americans."[44]

—Charmaine Riley, communications director of the Leadership Conference on Civil and Human Rights

strict voter ID laws and stop the drastic reduction in the number of polling places in some states. As the communications director of the Leadership Conference on Civil and Human Rights, Charmaine Riley, explains, the law is meant to restore and strengthen the Voting Rights Act: "The John Lewis Voting Rights Advancement Act would help identify barriers that could silence Black, Hispanic, Indigenous, young and new Americans and ensure we all have an equal say in the decisions that impact our lives."[44] As of the winter of 2021, the Senate had taken no action on the bill.

For the People Act

The Lewis act was one of two election laws passed in the House in 2021. The other, known as the For the People Act, would institute many permanent changes to the way people vote in the United States. And it would override most voting and election restrictions recently enacted by state legislators.

The For the People Act would make it easy for Americans to register to vote no matter where they live by offering online voter registration for federal elections. This is meant to address the fact that one in four eligible voters in the United States are not registered, the lowest voter participation rates of any modern democracy. Elections experts say that states that offer online registration up to the day of election show increased registration rates.

According to the National Association for the Advancement of Colored People (NAACP) Legal Defense and Educational Fund, Delaware processes over 80 percent of new registrations online, compared to less than 40 percent nationally. This can be compared to Texas, where, according to the *Texas Tribune,* it is harder to vote than any other state. Texas is one of only eight states that do not allow voters to register online. Voters have to visit their county voter registrar's office in person to register. Those who do not want to travel to their county office can obtain a mail-in registration application at a library, high school, or government office. According to the *Texas Tribune*, lack of online registration helps explain why Texas has one of the lowest voter turnout rates in the country, averaging around 50 percent in most elections.

The For the People Act contains another measure meant to increase voter participation among young people. The bill would institute what is called preregistration for high school juniors and seniors. Students who will reach the legal voting age of eighteen by the time of the next election could fill out registration forms marked as pending. Upon turning eighteen, the applicant would automatically be registered to vote.

Many states allow students to request preregistration, but in 2018 Oregon became the first to automatically register sixteen- and seventeen-year-olds when they get a driver's license. This accounted for a surge of young voters participating in elections

The John Lewis Voting Rights Advancement Act, named after late activist John Lewis (pictured at a 2017 rally), would protect the right to vote by forcing states with a history of voter discrimination to get approval before changing election laws.

once they turned eighteen. Oregon governor Kate Brown explains the importance of preregistration: "States like Georgia and Texas are passing voter suppression laws targeted at young people. In Oregon, I'm committed to ensuring every eligible young voter has an opportunity to have their voice heard. Young people have a vested interest in Oregon's future and should be able to register and cast their vote free from barriers."[45]

Opposing Views

The For the People Act contains provisions that provide national standards for voting and counting votes. It limits the way voter rolls can be purged, improves voting systems security, and provides guidelines for ballot collection. The bill has been opposed by most Republicans. Critics say the bill would weaken election security while giving the federal government too much power over state elections officials. Republican Senate minority leader Mitch McConnell expressed his disapproval: "What this is really about is an effort for the federal government to take over the way we conduct elections in this country. It is a solution in search of a problem."[46]

Despite McConnell's characterization of the proposed law as a power grab, the For the People Act is popular with the American public. When the polling organization Data for Progress explained the provisions of the bill to likely voters in a 2021 survey 67 percent said they supported its passage. This support crossed partisan lines: 56 percent of Republicans, 68 percent of Independents, and 77 percent of Democrats voiced support for the bill.

Executive Orders and Lawsuits

Voting rights activists were hoping that widespread public support would provide momentum in the fight for voting rights. But they were not waiting for congressional action to halt what they believe are efforts to suppress citizens from exercising their right to vote. Civil rights leaders and voting rights activists met with Joe Biden in 2021 to discuss what they view as a wave of anti-voter legislation

The For the People Act

When the For the People Act was passed in the House of Representatives in 2021, the bill spelled out voting problems and the powers Congress can wield over election laws. What follows is an excerpted section of the act:

Congress finds that the Constitution of the United States grants explicit and broad authority to protect the right to vote, to regulate elections for Federal office, to prevent and remedy discrimination in voting, and to defend the Nation's democratic process. Congress enacts the "For the People Act of 2021" pursuant to this broad authority. . . . Recent elections and studies have shown that minority communities wait longer in lines to vote, are more likely to have their mail ballots rejected, continue to face intimidation at the polls, are more likely to be disenfranchised by voter purges, and are disproportionately burdened by voter identification and other voter restrictions. Research shows that communities of color are more likely to face nearly every barrier to voting than their white counterparts. . . .

The ability of all eligible citizens of the United States to access and exercise their constitutional right to vote in a free, fair, and timely manner must be vigilantly enhanced, protected, and maintained.

John P. Sarbanes, "H.R. 1—For the People Act of 2021," Congress.gov, 2021. www.congress.gov.

being passed in states across the country. In that meeting activists said the president urged them to "out organize voter suppression."[47] This means registering more people to vote, ensuring they have proper ID, and taking other measures to get more voters to the polls. Wade Henderson, president of the Leadership Conference on Civil and Human Rights, attended the meeting. He says, "We intend to make mobilizations around the country a theme that we pursue. So this is not simply about sitting in our chairs waiting for the president to rescue the country. In this time of peril, we intend to be active participants in pressing Congress to act and then providing the kind of mobilization at the street level that will be essential to make it happen."[48] As part of this effort, the Democratic National Committee announced that it would spend $25 million to expand voting rights across the country.

These measures tie in with an executive order the president signed in March 2021 to promote voting rights. The order directs federal agencies to develop plans to promote voter registration and participation. As part of the order, citizens would be automatically registered to vote if they interact with federal agencies, including military recruiters, food stamp providers, and the government health care program known as Medicaid. Additionally, a special group was formed to expand voter turnout among Native American communities. As Biden said when he signed the executive order, "Every eligible voter should be able to vote and have that vote counted. . . . Let the people vote."[49] Groups like the League of Women Voters, the NAACP, and the American Federation of Teachers are at the forefront of this battle. They are lobbying and filing lawsuits to challenge discriminatory voter ID laws, unjust purges of voter rolls, and onerous voter registration processes.

Opponents of the sweeping election law overhaul in Texas filed a lawsuit almost immediately after the bill was enacted. The lawsuit argues that the new law is in violation of the Voting Rights

Across the United States, voting rights activists are taking action to fight against voter suppression. Here, a volunteer helps a woman in Austin, Texas, register to vote.

Calling for Biden to Take Action

In July 2021 Sherrilyn Ifill, president of the NAACP Legal Defense and Educational Fund, issued a public statement calling on Joe Biden and Congress to address threats to voting rights by passing the John Lewis Voting Rights Advancement Act and the For the People Act. Ifill stated:

> The right to vote is the cornerstone of our democracy—and ensuring equal, unfettered access to the ballot box for all eligible voters is critical to preserving the democratic values enshrined in our Constitution and built into our institutions. We commend President Biden for recognizing the perilousness of the threats to this fundamental right—particularly for voters of color—and the imminent danger they pose to the soundness of our democracy.

> Ifill argues that federal legislation is needed to ensure the right to vote for all eligible citizens. She says, "Anything less will result in the continued undermining of our democratic institutions—and will allow unacceptable threats to Black citizenship, voting, and political participation to continue unabated. . . . Congress must swiftly meet its obligation to uphold the principles of democracy—and do everything in its power to protect the fundamental right to vote."

Sherrilyn Ifill, "LDF Issues Statement on President Biden's Voting Rights Address," NAACP Legal Defense and Educational Fund, July 13, 2021. www.naacpldf.org.

Act and that it was purposely written to disenfranchise people of color. Similar lawsuits were filed in Georgia, Arizona, and elsewhere. Additional lawsuits were filed against Texas and Georgia by the US Department of Justice. As US attorney general Merrick Garland announced when filing the Georgia lawsuit, "The right of all eligible citizens to vote is the central pillar of our democracy, the right from which all other rights ultimately flow. This lawsuit is the first step of many we are taking to ensure that all eligible voters can cast a vote; that all lawful votes are counted; and that every voter has access to accurate information."[50]

Most Americans agree with Garland that all lawful votes should be counted and that no eligible voter should be turned away from the polls. In reality, securing voting rights in the United States has never been easy. And with around half the states passing restrictive election laws in 2021, this seems to be only the beginning.

SOURCE NOTES

Introduction: A Bitter Divide

1. Quoted in Madison Troyer, "Top Trump Tweets Since Election Day 2020," Stacker, December 30, 2020. https://stacker.com.
2. Quoted in Annika Kim Constantino, "Biden Condemns Trump's 'Big Lie' in Major Voting Rights Speech in Philadelphia," CNBC, July 12, 2021. www.cnbc.com.
3. Quoted in Jen Kirby, "Trump's Own Officials Say 2020 Was America's Most Secure Election in History," Vox, November 13, 2020. www.vox.com.
4. Quoted in Elise Viebeck and Eva Ruth Moravec, "Here's How the New Texas Voting Bill Will Affect Access to the Polls," *Washington Post*, August 31, 2021. www.washingtonpost.com.
5. Quoted in Viebeck and Moravec, "Here's How the New Texas Voting Bill Will Affect Access to the Polls."
6. Quoted in Ronald Brownstein, "Why Republican Voter Restrictions Are a Race Against Time," CNN, March 23, 2021. www.cnn.com.
7. Quoted in Monmouth University, "Public Supports Both Early Voting and Requiring Photo ID to Vote," June 21, 2021. www.monmouth.edu.

Chapter One: Voting Rights in the United States

8. Sean McElwee, "Why Voting Matters," Demos, September 16, 2015. www.demos.org.
9. John Lewis, "The Voting Rights Act: Ensuring Dignity and Democracy," *Human Rights*, Spring 2005, vol. 32, no. 2. www.americanbar.org.
10. Lewis, "The Voting Rights Act."
11. Lyndon B. Johnson, "Remarks in the Capitol Rotunda at the Signing of the Voting Rights Act," American Presidency Project. www.presidency.ucsb.edu.
12. Lewis, "The Voting Rights Act."
13. Quoted in Nina Totenberg, "Supreme Court: Congress Has to Fix Broken Voting Rights Act," *All Things Considered*, NPR, June 25, 2013. www.npr.org.

14. Barack Obama, "Statement by the President on the Supreme Court Ruling on *Shelby County v. Holder*," White House, June 25, 2013. https://obamawhitehouse.archives.gov.

Chapter Two: Ballot Barriers

15. Alexander Keyssar, *The Right to Vote: The Contested History of Democracy in the United States*. New York: Basic Books, 2009, p. 128.
16. Quoted in Philip Bump, "Yet Again, Trump Falsely Blames Illegal Voting for Getting Walloped in California," *Washington Post*, July 23, 2019. www.washingtonpost.com.
17. Quoted in Masood Farivar, "How Widespread Is Voter Fraud in the US?," Voice of America, September 13, 2020. www.voanews.com.
18. Quoted in Reid J. Epstein and Stephanie Saul, "Trump Says Mail Voting Means Republicans Would Lose Every Election. Is That True? No.," *Chicago Tribune*, April 10, 2020. www.chicagotribune.com.
19. Nathaniel Rakich and Jasmine Mithani, "What Absentee Voting Looked like in All 50 States," FiveThirtyEight, February 9, 2021. https://fivethirtyeight.com.
20. Quoted in Mark Scolforo and Colleen Long, "In Blistering Ruling, Judge Throws Out Trump Suit in PA," AP News, November 21, 2020. https://apnews.com.
21. Adeel Hassan, "What's in Florida's New Voting Law?," *New York Times*, May 10, 2021. www.nytimes.com.
22. Quoted in Amy Gardner, "Florida Republicans Rushed to Curb Mail Voting After Trump's Attacks on the Practice. Now Some Fear It Could Lower GOP Turnout," *Washington Post*, May 3, 2021. www.washingtonpost.com.
23. Quoted in Adrian Horton, "John Oliver: 'We Need to End the Filibuster' to Protect Voting Rights," *The Guardian* (Manchester, UK), September 27, 2021. www.theguardian.com.
24. Quoted in Philip Bump, "Group That Can't Find Systemic Voter Fraud Eager to Help Combat Systemic Voter Fraud," *Washington Post*, May 14, 2021. www.washingtonpost.com.
25. Quoted Ari Berman and Nick Surgey, "Leaked Video: Dark Money Groups Brag About Writing GOP Voter Suppression Bills Across the Country," *Mother Jones*, May 13, 2021. www.motherjones.com.
26. Quoted in Bill Barrow and Hilary Powell, "AP Interview: Stacey Abrams on Voting Rights, Her Next Move," AP News, April 9, 2021. https://apnews.com.

27. Quoted in Fredreka Schouten et al., "'Cannot Wait for Washington': How Voting Rights Activists Are Navigating New Restrictions Ahead of November Elections," CNN, October 11, 2021. www.cnn.com.

Chapter Three: Polling Place Pressures

28. Quoted in APM Reports, "After the Purge," October 29, 2019. www.apmreports.org.
29. Quoted in Matthew Rozsa, "This Website Will Tell Georgia Voters If They Were Purged . . . but They Must Reregister by Tuesday," Salon, October 7, 2018. www.salon.com.
30. Quoted in Geoff Hing et al., "Georgia Purged About 107,000 People from Voter Rolls: Report," WABE, October 19, 2018. www.wabe.org.
31. Quoted in Jessica Taylor, "Georgia's Stacey Abrams Admits Defeat, Says Kemp Used 'Deliberate' Suppression to Win," NPR, November 16, 2018. www.npr.org.
32. Quoted in Paul J. Weber, "In Texas, GOP Voting Bills Zero In on Democratic Houston," AP News, April 15, 2021. https://apnews.com.
33. Quoted in Stephen Fowler, "Why Do Nonwhite Georgia Voters Have to Wait in Line for Hours? Too Few Polling Places," KPBS, October 17, 2020. www.npr.org.
34. Quoted in Sam Levine, "More than 10-Hour Wait and Long Lines as Early Voting Starts in Georgia," The Guardian (Manchester, UK), October 12, 2020. www.theguardian.com.
35. Quoted in Peter Eisler, "Two Georgia Election Workers Sue Far-Right Websites over False Fraud Allegations," Reuters, December 2, 2021. www.reuters.com.
36. Quoted in Anthony Izaguirre, "Exodus of Election Officials Raises Concerns of Partisanship," AP News, June 13, 2021. https://apnews.com.
37. Quoted in Jordan Williams, "Majority More Concerned About Voting Access than Fraud: Poll," The Hill (Washington, DC), July 2, 2021. https://thehill.com.

Chapter Four: Overcoming Legal Obstacles

38. Quoted in Laurel Morales, "For Navajo Nation in Arizona, the Election Process Is Complicated and Problematic," NPR, June 29, 2020. www.npr.org.
39. Quoted in Morales, "For Navajo Nation in Arizona, the Election Process Is Complicated and Problematic."

40. Quoted in Ballotpedia, "Arguments for and Against Ballot Harvesting/Ballot Collection," 2019. https://ballotpedia.org.

41. Quoted in Native American Rights Fund, "9th Circuit Declares Arizona Voting Restriction to Be Discriminatory," January 27, 2020. www.narf.org.

42. Quoted in Linda Greenhouse, "On Voting Rights, Justice Alito Is Stuck in the 1980s," *New York Times*, July 15, 2021. www.nytimes.com.

43. Quoted in John Kruzel, "Supreme Court Leaves Arizona Voting Restrictions in Place," *The Hill* (Washington, DC), July 1, 2021. https://thehill.com.

44. Charmaine Riley, "Democracy in Peril, John Lewis Voting Rights Advancement Act Would Provide Protection," Leadership Conference on Civil and Human Rights, October 5, 2021. https://civilrights.org.

45. Quoted in KTVZ, "Report: Oregon's Millennial Voter Registration Soars," February 21, 2019. https://ktvz.com.

46. Quoted in Barbara Sprunt, "Senate Republicans Block Democrats' Sweeping Voting Rights Legislation," NPR, June 22, 2021. www.npr.org.

47. Quoted in Katie Rogers and Nick Corasaniti, "Democrats' Divide on Voting Rights Widens as Biden Faces Pressure," *New York Times*, July 22, 2021. www.nytimes.com.

48. Quoted in Matt Viser, "Civil Rights Leaders Dial Up Pressure on White House to Protect Voting Rights," *Washington Post*, July 8, 2021. www.washingtonpost.com.

49. Quoted in Donald Judd and Devan Cole, "Bidden Signs Executive Order Expanding Voting Access," CNN, March 7, 2021. www.cnn.com.

50. Quoted in US Department of Justice, "Justice Department Files Lawsuit Against the State of Georgia to Stop Racially Discriminatory Provisions of New Voting Law," June 25, 2021. www.justice.gov.

FOR FURTHER RESEARCH

Books

Judy Dodge Cummings, *Changing Laws: Politics of the Civil Rights Era*. Norwich, VT: Nomad, 2020.

John Lewis et al., *March* (trilogy). Marietta, GA: Top Shelf, 2016.

New York Times Editorial Staff, ed., *Voter Suppression: Blocking the Ballot Box.* New York: New York Times Educational Publishing, 2020.

Susan Goldman Rubin, *Give Us the Vote! Over Two Hundred Years of Fighting for the Ballot.* New York: Holiday House, 2021.

Diane C. Taylor, *Sitting In, Standing Up: Leaders of the Civil Rights Era*. Norwich, VT: Nomad, 2020.

Internet Sources

Bill Barrow and Hilary Powell, "AP Interview: Stacey Abrams on Voting Rights, Her Next Move," AP News, April 9, 2021. https://apnews.com.

Ari Berman and Nick Surgey, "Leaked Video: Dark Money Groups Brag About Writing GOP Voter Suppression Bills Across the Country," *Mother Jones*, May 13, 2021. www.motherjones.com.

Brennan Center for Justice, "Annotated Guide to the For the People Act of 2021," March 18, 2021. www.brennancenter.org.

Hillary Rodham Clinton, "The Fight for Voting Rights Is the Fight for Our Democracy," Democracy Docket, July 7, 2021. www.democracy docket.com.

Merrick Garland, "It Is Time for Congress to Act Again to Protect the Right to Vote," *Washington Post*, August 5, 2021. www.washington post.com.

Barack Obama, "Statement by the President on the Supreme Court Ruling on *Shelby County v. Holder*," White House, June 25, 2013. https://obamawhitehouse.archives.gov.

Websites

Brennan Center for Justice
www.brennancenter.org
The Brennan Center for Justice is a nonpartisan organization dedicated to democracy and equal justice. The center is one of the leading institutions defending voting rights and fighting efforts to purge voter rolls, shut down polling places, and disenfranchise minority voters.

Heritage Foundation
www.heritage.org
Founded in 1973, the Heritage Foundation is a research and educational institution that seeks to formulate and promote conservative public policies. The foundation tracks election integrity in every state and provides details about every case of voter fraud committed over the decades.

League of Women Voters
www.lwv.org
The League of Women Voters is a nonpartisan organization committed to helping women gain a larger role in political affairs. The league lobbies against voter ID laws, works to make voter registration easier, and supports efforts to extend the franchise to ex-felons and others shut out of the voting process.

National Association for the Advancement of Colored People (NAACP) Legal Defense and Educational Fund
www.naacpldf.org
The Legal Defense and Educational Fund is the legal arm of the NAACP civil rights organization, which fights for racial justice through litigation, advocacy, and public education. The fund focuses on criminal justice reform, economic equality, and ending restrictions on voting rights.

National Vote at Home Institute (NVAHI)
https://voteathome.org
The mission of the nonpartisan NVAHI is to expand voting options by making absentee ballots available to all Americans. The website features petitions, policy papers, social media tool kits, and other materials for community activists, election officials, and lawmakers.

Public Interest Legal Foundation (PILF)
https://publicinterestlegal.org
PILF is a conservative organization that works to fight fraud in American elections by ensuring voter rolls are cleansed of double voters and deceased citizens. The foundation files lawsuits against election officials to force them to disclose alleged noncitizen voter records.

INDEX

PICTURE CREDITS

ABOUT THE AUTHOR

Stuart A. Kallen is the author of more than 350 nonfiction books for children and young adults. He has written on topics ranging from the theory of relativity to the art of electronic dance music. In 2018 Kallen won a Green Earth Book Award from the Nature Generation environmental organization for his book *Trashing the Planet: Examining the Global Garbage Glut*. In his spare time he is a singer, songwriter, and guitarist in San Diego.